THE CASE FOR OPEN SPACE

WHY THE REAL ESTATE INDUSTRY SHOULD INVEST IN PARKS AND OPEN SPACES

ABOUT THIS REPORT

The Urban Land Institute
The Urban Land Institute is a global, member-driven organization comprising more than 42,000 real estate and urban development professionals dedicated to advancing the Institute's mission of providing leadership in the responsible use of land and in creating and sustaining thriving communities worldwide.

ULI's interdisciplinary membership represents all aspects of the industry, including developers, property owners, investors, architects, urban planners, public officials, real estate brokers, appraisers, attorneys, engineers, financiers, and academics. Established in 1936, the Institute has a presence in the Americas, Europe, and Asia Pacific regions, with members in 80 countries.

More information is available at uli.org. Follow ULI on Twitter, Facebook, LinkedIn, and Instagram.

ULI Building Healthy Places Initiative
Around the world, communities face pressing health challenges related to the built environment. Through the Building Healthy Places Initiative, launched in 2013, ULI is leveraging the power of ULI's global networks to shape projects and places in ways that improve the health of people and communities. Learn more and connect with Building Healthy Places: www.uli.org/health.

ULI Sustainable Development Council
ULI product councils are groups of ULI members who meet regularly to share information and best practices. The Sustainable Development Council aims to accelerate the adoption and implementation of sustainability, resilience, and health across the real estate industry. The council provides a forum for exchange of emerging best practices, including planning, financing, entitlements, design, construction, and operational aspects of projects that advance triple-bottom-line benefits while fostering more sustainable built environments.

Report Background
The Case for Open Space explores the benefits of private sector involvement in creating, maintaining, operating, and programming parks and open space—ranging from enhanced returns on investment for developers that include open space in their projects to improved community health outcomes.

This publication by the Urban Land Institute's Building Healthy Places Initiative and Sustainable Development Council (SDC) incorporates research conducted by ULI staff and SDC members, as well as takeaways from stakeholder interviews—including with ULI members who have developed or supported parks and open space through their project investments.

Support for this research was provided by the Robert Wood Johnson Foundation. The views expressed here do not necessarily reflect the views of the Foundation.

REPORT TEAM

ULI Sustainable Development Council

Elizabeth Shreeve
Principal, SWA Group
Chair, Sustainable Development Council

Chris Dunn
Principal, Dunn + Kiley
Founder, Cordis Certified Healthy

James F. Lima
President, James Lima Planning + Development

Project Leads

Matthew Norris
Senior Manager, Content

Reema Singh
Senior Associate, Content

ULI Project Staff

Rachel MacCleery
Senior Vice President, Content

Billy Grayson
Executive Director, Center for Sustainability and Economic Performance

Bridget Stesney
Senior Director, Content

James A. Mulligan
Senior Editor

Laura Glassman, Publications Professionals LLC
Manuscript Editor

Brandon Weil
Art Director

Anne Morgan
Lead Graphic Designer

Katteh Tongol Wong
Creative Consultant, PurpleCircle Design (Singapore)

Jes-Sy Ong
Senior Graphic Designer, PurpleCircle Design (Singapore)

Craig Chapman
Senior Director, Publishing Operations

ULI Senior Executives

Ed Walter
Global Chief Executive Officer

Adam Smolyar
Chief Marketing and Membership Officer

Cheryl Cummins
Global Governance Officer

John Fitzgerald
Chief Executive Officer, ULI Asia Pacific

Lisette van Doorn
Chief Executive Officer, ULI Europe

Michael Terseck
Chief Financial Officer/Chief Administrative Officer

Steve Ridd
Executive Vice President, Global Business Operations

> Active open spaces are proven to deliver an excellent return on investment, often supplying far more in benefits than they cost to construct. These benefits accrue to private development while effectively strengthening communities and opening opportunities for all.

Elizabeth Shreeve
Principal, SWA Group; chair, ULI Sustainable Development Council

San Jacinto Plaza | El Paso, Texas
Jonnu Singleton

CONTENTS

PART 1

INTRODUCTION

❝ The addition of open-space elements that encourage a healthy lifestyle creates a compelling story that differentiates a development and provides a competitive advantage. This can result in faster lease-ups or sales absorption as well as loyalty to the project, leading to increased tenant retention. ❞

Chris Dunn
Principal, Dunn + Kiley; founder, Cordis Certified Healthy; member, ULI Sustainable Development Product Council

Moxy Denver Cherry Creek | Denver, Colorado
Cherry Creek Beer Garden

A MESSAGE FROM THE ULI SUSTAINABLE DEVELOPMENT COUNCIL

Parks and open spaces are essential for the creation of vibrant communities and successful projects. As practitioners and investors, we may well realize this: But how can we identify specific opportunities to incorporate various types of open spaces into our projects? How can we better understand both the health benefits and the return on investment? Who should build them? Who should maintain them? Where are the evidence, the lessons learned, and the proven case studies?

With these questions in mind, we have been delighted to undertake *the Case for Open Space* in collaboration with ULI's Building Healthy Places Initiative. Our Sustainable Development Council members care deeply about connecting sustainable practices for health and resilience with the business of real estate.

As developers, designers, and technical experts, we understand the importance of high-quality outdoor places for congregation, exercise, active transportation, and connection to nature. We also note the ever-increasing role of the private sector in building, operating, and maintaining community-accessible open space—especially in the face of constrained government budgets and the often slow pace of public capital projects. Fortunately, developers can collaborate with communities to address local needs and support healthy lifestyles, while amplifying returns on investment for their projects.

The topic of health and public space rests on an honorable legacy. Urban parks long ago earned a reputation as the "lungs of the city." As urban planning and public health emerged together in the 19th and 20th centuries, visionaries such as Frederick Law Olmsted posited the essential role of open green space for controlling disease. Since then, the two fields have diverged into separate disciplines of architecture and medicine—only to be brought together again more recently, through the efforts of ULI and other leadership groups, into a growing global dialogue on health and the built environment.

This report aims to provide a range of ideas and inspirations for owners and real estate developers as they consider whether and how to invest in the public realm. We regard this as an initial step, with more specific tools and strategies to follow. As a first pass, however, the study points to a winning formula: when undertaken thoughtfully, the creation of privately owned or operated, community-accessible open spaces can provide equitable access to resources, strengthen communities, reduce execution risk, and contribute to a solid bottom line for real estate investment.

Elizabeth Shreeve
Principal, SWA Group
Chair, ULI Sustainable Development Council

Chris Dunn
Principal, Dunn + Kiley
Founder, Cordis Certified Healthy
Member, ULI Sustainable Development Council

James Lima
President, James Lima Planning + Development
Member, ULI Sustainable Development Council

> ❝ Recent public/private partnerships to create publicly accessible open space, such as Domino Park in Williamsburg, Brooklyn, demonstrate the enormous value to both public and private interests of a savvy real estate developer investing in new placemaking of the highest design caliber and meaningfully engaging with diverse groups from the local community about programming and activation of these spaces. ❞

James Lima
President, James Lima Planning + Development;
member ULI Sustainable Development Council

Domino Park | Brooklyn, New York
Daniel Levin

THE VALUE OF PRIVATE INVESTMENT IN OPEN SPACE

Parks and open spaces provide substantial benefits for individuals and communities, yet public resources to create and operate these spaces are limited. Increasingly, owners and developers are filling the gap by building, operating, or funding open spaces—with positive implications for community health, environmental sustainability, and real estate project success.

A survey of successful project examples from across the United States indicates that investing in high-quality, vibrant open spaces can pay dividends. Such places include a range of small to moderately scaled spaces—from pocket parks to trails and downtown parks—where people can gather, play, exercise, and relax with friends, family, and neighbors.

Opportunities to leverage demand for such spaces are significant: 85 percent of U.S. residents identify proximity to parks, playgrounds, open space, or recreation centers as an important factor in their decision of where to live.[1] Yet public investment in park development and maintenance has remained stagnant or declined in recent years across the United States.[2,3]

In fact, many large U.S. cities have a substantial backlog in deferred maintenance for parks.[4] Estimates from 2018 suggest that New York City will need to invest $5.8 billion over the next decade to bring its parks to a state of good repair.[5]

Developer support can help bridge the gap between community needs and available public resources for parks and open spaces, especially for highly programmed parks in urban areas with intensive capital and operational demands.

Including open space and parks as part of a development project creates a win–win scenario for the community and the developer's return on investment. Oftentimes, well-used gathering spaces can be added in small or underutilized project areas and can be relatively inexpensive in the overall project context.

When combined with sustained public funding and efforts to ensure that investments in high-quality parks and open spaces are equitably distributed, private sector contributions to the creation and operation of these spaces can deliver results that benefit communities and developers alike.

Farmers Park, The Packing District | Anaheim, California
Chet Frohlich, 2015

RESEARCH APPROACH

To closely examine the value proposition for real estate involvement in the development and operations of community-accessible open space, ULI researchers identified roughly 30 open-space projects across the United States that members from the private sector support in a variety of ways.

Because open space has no standard definition, this report encompasses a variety of project types and scales, including pocket parks smaller than 0.25 acre (0.1 ha), linear parks that stretch over 3.5 miles (5.6 km), and neighborhood parks larger than 11 acres (4.5 ha).

Researchers purposefully selected a subset of these projects for interviews with project leaders, which explored how mechanisms related to partnerships, funding, zoning, and local engagement allowed developers to support project success while delivering significant community benefits. Through multiple conversations with industry experts, ULI identified four broad ways developers acquired benefits from investing in parks and open space that present a "win-win" for development and communities. Project examples help illustrate these four cases.

The research team also conducted a scan of peer-reviewed studies to uncover the latest empirical evidence on the comprehensive health and financial benefits of parks and open space. Findings from this research are highlighted in research briefs throughout the report.

Future ULI research will further examine best practices, mechanisms, and strategies to maximize the benefits of developer involvement in creation and operation of parks and open space.

Perk Park | Cleveland, Ohio
Lisa DeJong

Examples of Private Sector–Supported Open Spaces

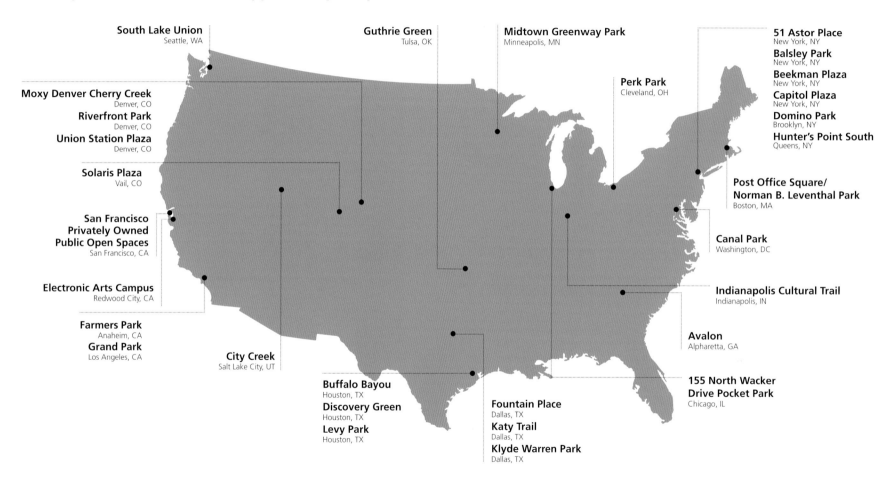

South Lake Union
Seattle, WA

Guthrie Green
Tulsa, OK

Midtown Greenway Park
Minneapolis, MN

51 Astor Place
New York, NY

Balsley Park
New York, NY

Beekman Plaza
New York, NY

Perk Park
Cleveland, OH

Capitol Plaza
New York, NY

Moxy Denver Cherry Creek
Denver, CO

Riverfront Park
Denver, CO

Union Station Plaza
Denver, CO

Domino Park
Brooklyn, NY

Hunter's Point South
Queens, NY

Solaris Plaza
Vail, CO

**Post Office Square/
Norman B. Leventhal Park**
Boston, MA

**San Francisco
Privately Owned
Public Open Spaces**
San Francisco, CA

Canal Park
Washington, DC

Electronic Arts Campus
Redwood City, CA

Indianapolis Cultural Trail
Indianapolis, IN

Farmers Park
Anaheim, CA

Grand Park
Los Angeles, CA

Avalon
Alpharetta, GA

City Creek
Salt Lake City, UT

**155 North Wacker
Drive Pocket Park**
Chicago, IL

Buffalo Bayou
Houston, TX

Discovery Green
Houston, TX

Levy Park
Houston, TX

Fountain Place
Dallas, TX

Katy Trail
Dallas, TX

Klyde Warren Park
Dallas, TX

Examples of Private Sector–Supported Open Spaces

51 Astor Place
New York, NY
Size: 0.1 acre (0.04 ha)
Cost: $1.5 million
Project Type: New York City Privately Owned Public Space

Avalon
Alpharetta, GA
Size: 0.23 acre (0.09 ha)
Project Type: Plaza/Open Space

Balsley Park
New York, NY
Size: 0.25 acre (0.10 ha)
Cost: $1 million
Project Type: New York City Privately Owned Public Space

Beekman Plaza
New York, NY
Size: 0.07 acre (0.03 ha)
Cost: $2.7 million
Project Type: New York City Privately Owned Public Space

Buffalo Bayou
Houston, TX
Size: 160 acres (64.75 ha); 2.3 miles (3.7 km)
Cost: $58 million
Project Type: Linear Park/Trail

Canal Park
Washington, DC
Size: 3 acres (1.21 ha)
Cost: $20 million
Project Type: Urban Park

Capitol Plaza
New York, NY
Size: 0.25 acre (0.10 ha)
Cost: $2 million
Project Type: New York City Privately Owned Public Space

City Creek
Salt Lake City, UT
Size: 2.07 acres (0.84 ha)
Cost: $55 million
Project Type: Plaza/Open Space

Discovery Green
Houston, TX
Size: 12 acres (4.86 ha)
Project Type: Urban Park

Domino Park
Brooklyn, NY
Size: 5 acres (2.02 ha)
Cost: $50 million
Project Type: Urban Park

Electronic Arts Campus
Redwood City, CA
Size: ~31 acres (12.55 ha)
Cost: $3.6 million
Project Type: Plaza/Open Space

Farmers Park
Anaheim, CA
Size: 2 acres (0.81 ha)
Project Type: Urban Park

Fountain Place
Dallas, TX
Size: ~5.5 acres (2.23 ha)
Project Type: Plaza/Open Space

Grand Park
Los Angeles, CA
Size: 12 acres (4.9 ha)
Cost: $50 million
Project Type: Urban Park

Guthrie Green
Tulsa, OK
Size: 2.6 acres (1.05 ha)
Cost: $8.6 million
Project Type: Urban Park

Hunter's Point South
Queens, NY
Size: 11 acres (4.5 ha)
Cost: $160 million
Project Type: Urban Park

Indianapolis Cultural Trail
Indianapolis, IN
Size: 8 miles (13 km)
Cost: $62.5 million
Project Type: Linear Park/Trail

Katy Trail
Dallas, TX
Size: 3.5 miles (5.6 km)
Cost: $23 million
Project Type: Linear Park/Trail

Klyde Warren Park
Dallas, TX
Size: 5 acres (2.02 ha)
Cost: $112 million
Project Type: Urban Park

Levy Park
Houston, TX
Size: 5.9 acres (2.39 ha)
Cost: $15 million
Project Type: Urban Park

Midtown Greenway Park
Minneapolis, MN
Size: 5.5 miles (8.8 km)
Cost: $36 million
Project Type: Linear Park/Trail

Moxy Denver Cherry Creek
Denver, CO
Size: <0.25 acre (0.20 ha)
Project Type: Plaza/Open Space

155 North Wacker Drive Pocket Park
Chicago, IL
Size: 0.21 acre (0.08 ha)
Cost: $1.5 million
Project Type: Plaza/Open Space

Perk Park
Cleveland, OH
Size: ~1 acre (0.40 ha)
Cost: $3 million
Project Type: Urban Park

Post Office Square/ Norman B. Leventhal Park
Boston, MA
Size: 1.7 acres (0.69 ha)
Cost: $80 million
Project Type: Urban Park

Riverfront Park
Denver, CO
Size: 2.2 acres (0.89 ha)
Project Type: Urban Park

San Francisco Privately Owned Public Open Spaces
San Francisco, CA
Size: Varied: <1 acre (0.40 ha)
Cost: $1 million
Project Type: Privately Owned Public Space

Solaris Plaza
Vail, CO
Size: 0.7 acre (0.28 ha)
Cost: $15 million
Project Type: Plaza/Open Space

South Lake Union
Seattle, WA
Size: 12 acres (4.86 ha)
Project Type: Urban Park

Union Station Wynkoop Plaza
Denver, CO
Size: 0.69 acre (0.28 ha)
Project Type: Plaza/Open Space

DEVELOPER ROLES AND BENEFITS

How Developers Support Open Space

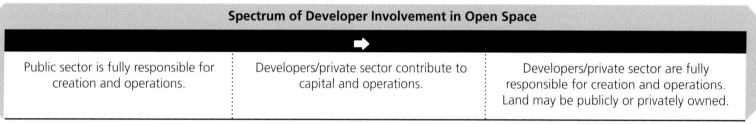

Spectrum of Developer Involvement in Open Space

Public sector is fully responsible for creation and operations.	Developers/private sector contribute to capital and operations.	Developers/private sector are fully responsible for creation and operations. Land may be publicly or privately owned.

Examples of Developer Roles in the Creation and Operation of Open Space

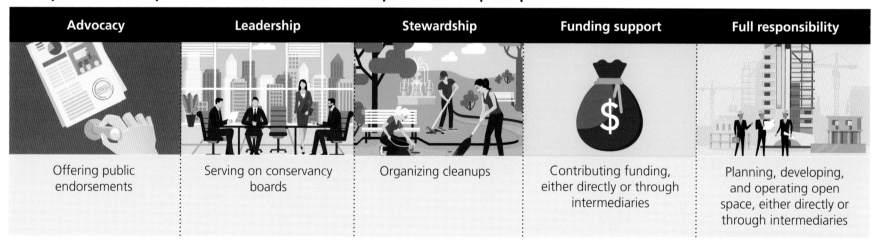

Advocacy	Leadership	Stewardship	Funding support	Full responsibility
Offering public endorsements	Serving on conservancy boards	Organizing cleanups	Contributing funding, either directly or through intermediaries	Planning, developing, and operating open space, either directly or through intermediaries

Potential Benefits to Developers of Supporting Community-Accessible Open Space

By Phase of Real Estate Development

Planning and design	Project marketing	Project completion	Operations and maintenance (O&M)

• Stronger support for proposed developments through early community engagement on open-space components
 	
• Increased buy-in from influential stakeholders, including public officials and investors
 	
• Faster zoning approvals and entitlements from local jurisdictions, lowering project costs
 	
• Increased development size or density in localities with park/open-space zoning incentives
 	
• Enhanced likelihood of winning RFPs to develop projects because of civic contributions
	• Ability to capture strong market demand for parks and open space
	
	• Increased marketability due to project differentiation
	
	• Ability to enhance project branding or burnish a firm's reputation through high-quality design
	
	• Opportunities for public recognition through sponsored public events, awards, or iconic features
	
	• Increased project visibility because of foot traffic
		• Accelerated market absorption rates
		
		• Enhanced asset value through higher rent premiums, lower vacancy rates, or faster lease-ups
		
		• Ability to command sales or rental rates above comparable projects that lack open space
		
		• Economic development that supports project value through
		  – Job creation and business relocation and attraction
		  – Complementary neighborhood development/synergistic uses
		
		• Equitable development opportunities through partnerships on workforce development, small business retention, and affordable housing
			• Increased net operating income
			
			• New sources of revenue streams from vendors, concessions, or events to offset O&M costs
			
			• Long-term cost savings through resilience-promoting amenities
			
			• Better mortgage insurance rates from debt providers
			
			• Sustained value/future-proofing
			
			• Increased business for retail tenants, reducing vacancy and tenant turnover
			
			• Increased residential tenant retention
			
			• Long-term real estate value appreciation
			
			• Project resilience during economic downturns

PART 2

THE CASE FOR OPEN SPACE

> It's important for all stakeholders to work together to invest in places for the public to come together and be active. The Katy Trail is such a place. Partnerships with developers, such as JLB Partners—who built a new public access point to the trail—serve to further enhance community links to one of our city's best amenities.

Robin Baldock
Executive director, Friends of Katy Trail

Katy Trail | Dallas, Texas
Lauren Whitson

The following four cases present compelling reasons for developers to support open space. *The Case for Open Space* was developed through research with industry experts. Examples of developer-supported open-space projects as well as peer-reviewed research serve to further illustrate these cases.

Ultimately, *The Case for Open Space* conveys that through investments in open space, developers can provide needed community benefits, while maximizing opportunities to create residential, commercial, and mixed-use projects with near-term appeal and sustained, long-term value.

The Case for Developer-Supported Open Spaces

01 By investing in equitable access to parks and open space, developers can help **improve community health and wellness, boost economic development,** and enhance a project's **financial success**.

02 Developer-supported parks and open spaces can **help mitigate** the impact of insufficient public resources for parks, thereby providing communities with **access to beneficial open space while enhancing long-term real estate value.**

03 Community-driven programming supported by the private sector can **activate open spaces, foster social interaction,** and strengthen the overall **value** and **marketability** of associated projects.

04 Creating or funding parks and open spaces can help developers secure **community buy-in, public sector support,** and valuable **zoning incentives** in communities where these incentives are available.

"The waterfront development at Hunter's Point South has demonstrated the power of open space—truly democratic common ground in which existing and new neighbors are connected to each other and their river."

Tom Balsley
Principal, SWA/Balsley

Hunter's Point South | Queens, New York
Jonnu Singleton, SWA Group

By investing in equitable access to parks and open space, developers can help **improve community health and wellness, boost economic development**, and enhance a project's **financial success**.

Challenge

To compete effectively in today's marketplace, developers and communities must invest in creating thriving communities that promote the health and well-being of all residents. Although parks and open spaces can enhance a community's quality of life and the financial success of development projects, one in three Americans do not have a park within a ten-minute walk (or half-mile) of home.[6]

Solution

Developer investment in parks and open spaces that include features such as green infrastructure, playgrounds, fitness equipment, and culturally relevant programming can give developers and communities a competitive edge while enhancing values for adjacent properties. To ensure equitable open-space access and mitigate potential residential displacement, local stakeholders must work together to adopt inclusive development strategies from the start so all residents benefit from investment in parks and open space.

Potential Advantages

▲ Community support	▲ Buy-in from influential stakeholders	▲ Ability to meet market demand	▲ Equitable development opportunities	▲ Tenant retention

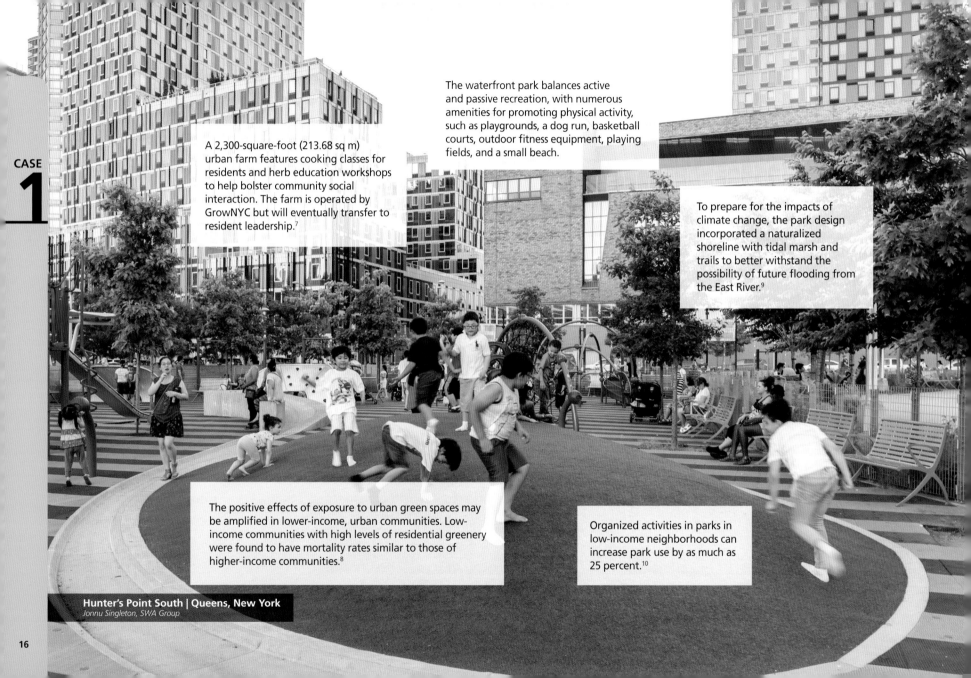

A 2,300-square-foot (213.68 sq m) urban farm features cooking classes for residents and herb education workshops to help bolster community social interaction. The farm is operated by GrowNYC but will eventually transfer to resident leadership.[7]

The waterfront park balances active and passive recreation, with numerous amenities for promoting physical activity, such as playgrounds, a dog run, basketball courts, outdoor fitness equipment, playing fields, and a small beach.

To prepare for the impacts of climate change, the park design incorporated a naturalized shoreline with tidal marsh and trails to better withstand the possibility of future flooding from the East River.[9]

The positive effects of exposure to urban green spaces may be amplified in lower-income, urban communities. Low-income communities with high levels of residential greenery were found to have mortality rates similar to those of higher-income communities.[8]

Organized activities in parks in low-income neighborhoods can increase park use by as much as 25 percent.[10]

Hunter's Point South | Queens, New York
Jonnu Singleton, SWA Group

HUNTER'S POINT SOUTH

When New York City set out to build its largest new affordable housing complex in more than three decades, a development team consisting of Related Companies, Phipps Houses, and Monadnock Construction was selected to build the first phase. This included 925 permanently affordable housing units, roughly 20,000 square feet (1,858 sq m) of new retail space, a new public school, a community facility space, and a waterfront park.

As part of land disposition agreements negotiated by the New York City Department of Housing Preservation and Development, project developers are required to provide annual payments to the New York City Department of Parks and Recreation to be used to help fund the waterfront park's maintenance.

As of 2018, the development's 11-acre (4.5 ha) park serves as a model for waterfront resilience and acts as a buffer against storm surges. Upon full completion, the Hunter's Point South development is anticipated to catalyze over $2 billion in private investment and create more than 4,600 jobs.[11]

Developers
Related Companies,
Phipps Houses,
and Monadnock
Construction

Designers
SWA/Balsley and
Weiss/Manfredi

Operations
New York City
Department
of Parks and
Recreation

Location
Queens, New York

Size of open space
11 acres (4.5 ha)

Project type
Mixed-use
affordable housing

Status
Park completed
in 2018

Cost
$360 million, with $160 million
for waterfront park[12]

> ❝ We know that there are racial disparities in rates of activity and childhood obesity, particularly in urban areas.…We have cross-sectional data from many studies that suggests people who live close to parks are more active, including children, and adolescents living near parks are less prone to being overweight.[13] ❞
>
> **Myron Floyd**
> PhD, professor and department head, Department of Parks, Recreation and Tourism Management at North Carolina State University

Canal Park | Washington, DC
OLIN / Sahar Coston-Hardy

HOW OPEN SPACES CAN PROMOTE EQUITABLE OUTCOMES

Over one-third of Americans (38 percent) say that their neighborhood lacks outdoor spaces to exercise—a barrier that disproportionately affects low-income African American and Latino communities.[14] When done right, such spaces can provide myriad benefits, including reducing rates of depression and increasing opportunities for people to engage in physical activity, especially within low-income communities.

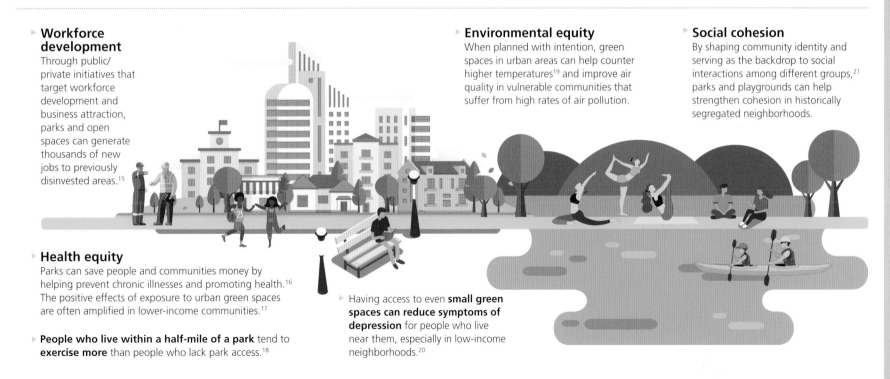

▷ Workforce development

Through public/ private initiatives that target workforce development and business attraction, parks and open spaces can generate thousands of new jobs to previously disinvested areas.[15]

▷ Environmental equity

When planned with intention, green spaces in urban areas can help counter higher temperatures[19] and improve air quality in vulnerable communities that suffer from high rates of air pollution.

▷ Social cohesion

By shaping community identity and serving as the backdrop to social interactions among different groups,[21] parks and playgrounds can help strengthen cohesion in historically segregated neighborhoods.

▷ Health equity

Parks can save people and communities money by helping prevent chronic illnesses and promoting health.[16] The positive effects of exposure to urban green spaces are often amplified in lower-income communities.[17]

▷ **People who live within a half-mile of a park** tend to **exercise more** than people who lack park access.[18]

▷ Having access to even **small green spaces can reduce symptoms of depression** for people who live near them, especially in low-income neighborhoods.[20]

> ❝ The public/private partnership between Midway and the city of Houston's Upper Kirby District Redevelopment Authority generates ongoing funding for park operations—a great benefit for the people in the surrounding area and an essential investment in the success of Midway's adjacent projects. ❞
>
> **Ann Taylor**
> Senior vice president, Midway

Levy Park | Houston, Texas
Dan Netz

Developer-supported parks and open spaces can help mitigate the impact of insufficient public resources for parks, thereby **providing communities with access to open space** while **enhancing long-term real estate value.**

Challenge

Many studies find significant increases—up to 40 percent[22]—in the value of properties adjacent to parks and open space. However, public investment in open-space creation, operations, programming, and upgrades has been flat or has declined in many places in recent years.[23] Poorly maintained parks can detract from the vibrancy and value of nearby commercial and residential properties.

Solution

Developers and building owners can provide funding for parks and open space through individual project investments or through financial contributions to intermediaries such as conservancies or business improvement districts. Steady revenue streams for public park and open-space operations can help transform underused public assets into accessible, vibrant, inclusive, and financially sustainable spaces that support follow-on neighborhood-serving development opportunities on adjacent land.

Potential Advantages

▲ Marketability	▲ Asset values	▲ Complementary neighborhood development	▲ Business for retail tenants	▲ Sustained value/ future-proofing

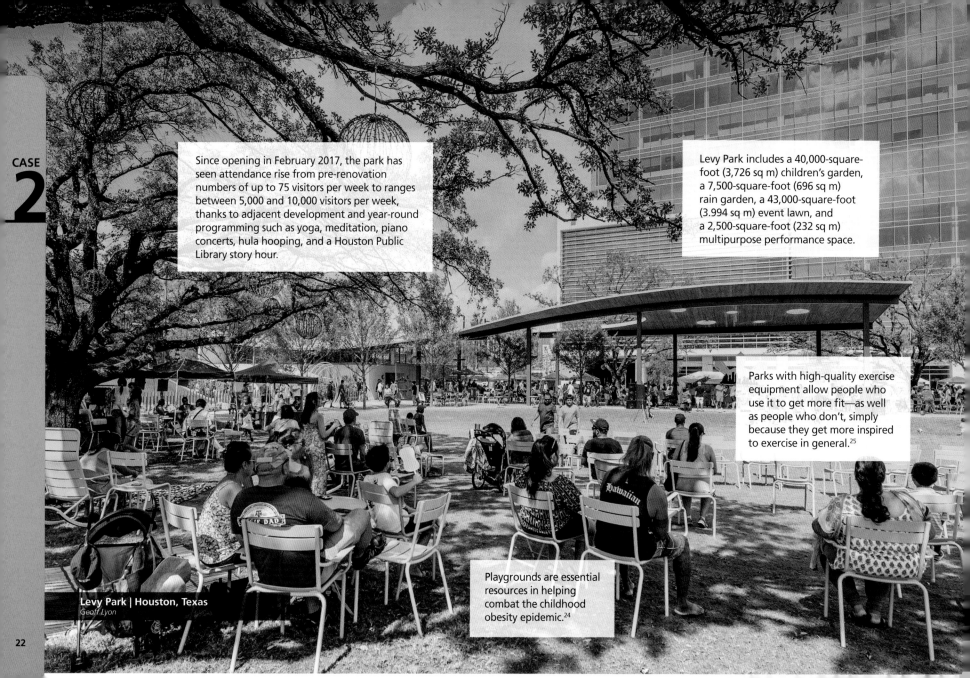

Since opening in February 2017, the park has seen attendance rise from pre-renovation numbers of up to 75 visitors per week to ranges between 5,000 and 10,000 visitors per week, thanks to adjacent development and year-round programming such as yoga, meditation, piano concerts, hula hooping, and a Houston Public Library story hour.

Levy Park includes a 40,000-square-foot (3,726 sq m) children's garden, a 7,500-square-foot (696 sq m) rain garden, a 43,000-square-foot (3.994 sq m) event lawn, and a 2,500-square-foot (232 sq m) multipurpose performance space.

Parks with high-quality exercise equipment allow people who use it to get more fit—as well as people who don't, simply because they get more inspired to exercise in general.[25]

Playgrounds are essential resources in helping combat the childhood obesity epidemic.[24]

Levy Park | Houston, Texas
Geoff Lyon

Levy Park is a 5.9-acre (2.39 ha) public park in Houston, Texas, that reopened in 2017 after a $15 million renovation that transformed it from an underused open space into the central component of an 11-acre (4.45 ha) urban activity center.

The park renovation—spearheaded by the Upper Kirby Redevelopment Authority (UKRA)—was completed with public funds, but maintenance is funded entirely through a partnership with Midway, a Houston-based real estate investment and development firm.

Midway signed two 99-year ground leases on UKRA-owned, park-adjacent land that allowed the development of Kirby Grove,

a 225,000-square-foot (20,903 sq m) office building with 25,000 square feet (2,323 sq m) of ground-floor restaurant space, and Avenue Grove, a 270-unit mid-rise residential tower.

UKRA assembled properties adjacent to Levy Park to improve park access and allow adjacent development, resulting in a nearly half-acre (0.2 ha) increase in park size and roughly five acres (2.02 ha) of adjacent developable land.

This innovative partnership unlocked new development opportunities for Midway and continues to support increased park patronage while generating the necessary funding for park operations.

Developer
Upper Kirby
Redevelopment
Authority

Designer
OJB Landscape
Architecture

Operations
Levy Park
Conservancy;
Midway
Companies

Location
Houston, Texas

Size of open space
5.9 acres (2.39 ha)

Project type
Public park;
maintenance
funded
through private
development

Status
Land originally deeded
to the city of Houston
in 1941; renovation
completed in 2017

Cost
$15 million park renovation

The bid package put together by the city and county of Los Angeles led to $50 million of private investment in Grand Park.

Grand Park was developed as a component of the Grand Avenue Plan, a public/private partnership to revitalize downtown Los Angeles's cultural and civic core with mixed-use and public spaces.

Many studies cite the calming effects of spending time in nature, and health can be harmed by a lack of exposure to nature.[26]

Grand Park hosts cultural events, music performances, festivals, and yoga and fitness classes.

Grand Park | Los Angeles, California
Jim Simmons; Rios Clementi Hale Studios; County of Los Angeles

Project Example

GRAND PARK

Related California funded $50 million in major upgrades to transform a formerly underused public space into Grand Park—a 12-acre (4.9 ha) public park in downtown Los Angeles. Related's commitment to developing the park led to city approval for a mixed-use project on adjacent publicly owned parcels.

Related and the Grand Avenue Committee hosted 12 community meetings to determine Grand Park's design, which they envisioned as

"the park for everyone." These meetings included translators to ensure that the diverse voices of Los Angeles residents were reflected in the final park design.

Related completed the park in 2012—well in advance of plans to move forward with its associated $1 billion mixed-used project, now scheduled to begin construction in 2018.

Developers
Related California and County of Los Angeles

Designers
Superjacent and Rios Clementi Hale Studios

Operations
Los Angeles Music Center

Location
Los Angeles, California

Size of open space
12 acres (4.9 ha)

Project type
Urban park funded through private development

Status
Completed in 2012

Cost
$50 million

> With its mixed-use development project on hold due to the recession, Related, having already provided the funds to the county, had the opportunity to focus its efforts and build Grand Park early. Related's efficiency in developing the park created an enormous amount of goodwill with L.A. County and the community overall—a significant benefit that allowed the development plans to proceed.

Tony Paradowski
Co-founder, Superjacent; board member, Grand Park Foundation

Grand Park | Los Angeles, California
Jim Simmons

THE DEMAND FOR MORE INVESTMENT IN OPEN SPACE

Investor support

79% of surveyed investors believe that open space can act as a "crucial catalyst for economic development."[27]

Of surveyed real estate developers, investors, consultants, and public sector workers, **84 percent** believe that "**both the public and private sectors should be responsible for the development of open spaces.**"[28]

Market demand

55% of U.S. residents say access to green space is a top or high priority when deciding where to live.[29]

Economic development

High-quality parks are one of the top factors that businesses cite in relocation decisions.[32]

Public support

83% of Americans believe they personally benefit from local parks.[33]

Funding need

Many large U.S. cities have a substantial backlog in deferred maintenance for parks.[30] Estimates from 2018 suggest that New York City will need to invest **$5.8 billion** over the next decade to bring its parks to a state of good repair.[31]

> **❝** Let us hope that Guthrie Green is a place that welcomes all, a place that binds up all of us—North and South and East and West; Christian, Muslim, and Jew; black and white; Hispanic; straight and gay; rich and poor and all in between—to talk and study, to listen and sing, to share, to explore, and to find joy. If so, we will have made an investment in the only asset that really matters—our people and our community—and that's an investment that will have a return for all. **❞**

Ken Levit
Executive director, George Kaiser Family Foundation

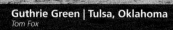

Guthrie Green | Tulsa, Oklahoma
Tom Fox

Community-driven programming supported by the private sector can **activate open spaces, foster social interaction**, and strengthen the overall **value** and **marketability** of associated projects.

Challenge

Even when developers invest in open space, optimal benefits for the project and the community will materialize only when those spaces are maintained and activated. In fact, sites that are not well programmed or maintained could engender adverse effects, where spaces intended for public use become underused and susceptible to vandalism.

Solution

Developers can contribute to open-space activation efforts in a range of ways—from providing financial support for community-driven programming to fully managing programming and operations, while still leveraging community input. Thoughtful programming can promote social interaction, community ownership, and pedestrian activity, boosting economic development and creating vibrant, thriving neighborhoods. These efforts strengthen project marketability.

Potential Advantages

- Community support
- Opportunities for public recognition
- Project visibility
- Retail sales
- Revenue streams from vendors

Committed to sustainability, the park contains a geo-exchange system that reduces energy demand by 60 percent to power nearby nonprofit centers.[34]

Guthrie Green's programs enhance community economic prosperity through increased property values, expansion of the local tax base, more tourism, and crime reduction.[35]

In 2017, Guthrie Green hosted over 400 community-driven events—ranging from protests to weddings to jazz concerts—attracting more than 300,000 visitors to the area.

Guthrie Green hosts a weekly market with fresh produce and locally prepared food, as well as free programs, including tai chi, yoga, fitness classes, and a premier three-day cycling festival.

The number of park users tends to increase with the presence of vendors, such as food carts.[36]

Guthrie Green | Tulsa, Oklahoma
Jonnu Singleton, SWA Group

GUTHRIE GREEN

Built and managed by the George Kaiser Family Foundation (GKFF), Guthrie Green transformed a 2.6-acre (1.05 ha) truck-loading facility into a vibrant, highly programmed urban park that now serves as a model for sustainability.

The foundation oversees ownership and maintenance of the park, including a robust community outreach process that invites all local residents, business owners, cultural organizations, and city officials to submit ideas for programming on a weekly basis.

The park has become the area's leading destination since its 2012 opening, drawing 3,000 people every week to daily activities and sparking $150 million in public/private investment to a variety of commercial and residential projects in the emerging 19-block Arts District of downtown Tulsa.[37]

Additional property investments by GKFF include reuse of historic buildings near the park for the Woody Guthrie Center, Bob Dylan Archive, and an arts–cultural museum complex.

Developer
George Kaiser
Family Foundation

Designer
SWA Group

Operations
George Kaiser
Family Foundation

Location
Tulsa, Oklahoma

Size of open space
2.6 acres (1.05 ha)

Project type
Urban park

Status
Completed in 2012

Cost
$8.5 million

The Plaza at Avalon | Alpharetta, Georgia
Josh Meister

PROGRAMMING IN PARKS

Research on Programming in Parks

- Parks that offer team sports activities, exercise classes, and other organized events are much more likely to be attended and used than those that do not include such offerings.[38]

- Organized activities in parks can increase park use by as much as 25 percent in low-income neighborhoods, where parks tend to be used less than parks in high-income neighborhoods.[39,40]

- In a nationwide study on parks, programming and marketing activities were associated with 37 percent and 63 percent more hours of moderate to vigorous physical activity per week, respectively.

Featured Project: Avalon | Alpharetta, Georgia

When creating Avalon, a $1 billion mixed-use development with 8.8 acres (3.6 ha) of gathering space, including a 10,000-square-foot (929 sq m) plaza, North American Properties (NAP) included a strong emphasis on placemaking and programming.[41]

The Plaza at Avalon | Alpharetta, Georgia
Josh Meister

▶ **Open space**
Open spaces include a linear park that features mature trees, a bocce court, a fire pit, seating areas, and a children's play area of **1,300-plus square feet (121 sq m)**.

▶ **Programming**
Avalon hosts more than **200 events** per year. NAP invests roughly three to four times more on programming than the typical developer.[42]

▶ **Project success**
In large part because of the programming at Avalon, project tenants have achieved retail sales exceeding **$1,000 per square foot**, single-family homes sell for **60 percent more** than budgeted sales prices, and the development has spurred the creation of more than **4,000 jobs.**

> **▎▎** The Community Development Department supported Solaris from the start, because plans for the mixed-use project included a public plaza capable of hosting special events of more than 6,500 people. We moved efficiently through the development review process, in part due to the developer's commitment to providing capital dollars for construction of the plaza. **▎▎**
>
> **George Ruther**
> Housing director and former director of community development, town of Vail

Solaris | Vail, Colorado
Solaris

Creating or funding parks and open spaces can help developers secure **community buy-in, public sector support**, and valuable **zoning incentives** in communities where these incentives are available.

Challenge

Without the appropriate land entitlements (zoning, use permits, landscaping, utility and road approvals), developers cannot proceed with projects. To receive necessary approvals, developers must demonstrate to local officials and residents that projects will benefit the surrounding community. Any delays in receiving approvals add to the costs of development.

Solution

By prioritizing the development, maintenance, or operation of parks and open space as part of an associated project, developers can garner public support (including from influential members of the community), be competitive in bidding for development opportunities on publicly controlled land, and more quickly receive the necessary approvals from public agencies to move projects forward. When local jurisdictions offer innovative zoning incentives for including open spaces as project components, developers may build larger, higher-density projects than would be permitted under traditional zoning.

Potential Advantages

▴ Buy-in from influential stakeholders	▴ Speed of zoning approvals	▴ Project cost savings	▴ Development density	▴ Likelihood of winning RFPs

Solaris Plaza, which can accommodate about 6,500 people at a time, hosts numerous small events and eight to ten marquee events annually, including concerts, athletic competitions, yoga, ice skating, sporting events, concerts, and community festivals.

Solaris includes 79 condominiums and 100,000 square feet (9,290 sq m) of commercial space.

Solaris Plaza has helped meet the town's objective of growing a year-round economy; the plaza features events nearly every weekend that support local economic development.

Parks tend to get more use when they are larger, have more facilities, offer more planned activities and events, and their services are marketed to the public.[43]

Parks with "fun" features such as skate parks or sport fields attract more people—and not just the people using those amenities.[44] Solaris Plaza features fountains in the summertime, fire pits in the winter, and specially commissioned public art sculptures.

Solaris | Vail, Colorado
Solaris

SOLARIS PLAZA

Solaris Plaza is a 30,000-square-foot (2,787 sq m) open space in Vail, Colorado, at the center of a 2.63-acre (1.06 ha) mixed-use project that replaced a surface parking lot and an aging shopping center.

The town of Vail allowed Solaris to be built at additional density and height because the project included an essential community gathering place.

Since opening in 2010, Solaris Plaza has become the central gathering place for residents and visitors to Vail and has hosted events ranging from a weekly farmers market to the GoPro Games.

Capital expenditures for the plaza were privately financed through the development of the larger Solaris project; the town of Vail operates the space and manages on-site programming through a business improvement district and easement, while the developer maintains the plaza.

Developer
Peter Knobel

Designers
Barnes Coy Architects,
Davis Partnership
Architects, SCI
Structural Engineers,
Jon Preach Boord
Enterprises, and
Flack & Kurtz

Operations
Plaza programmed
by town of Vail
under business
improvement
district/easement;
maintenance by
developer

Location
Vail, Colorado

Size of open space
Roughly 30,000 square feet (2,787 sq m)

Project type
Public plaza adjacent
to mixed-use
development

Status
Completed in 2010

Cost
$15 million for public plaza;
$325 million development

Municipalities now expect that every significant development will benefit the municipality in ways beyond attracting new residents or businesses. Those benefits may be traditional, such as infrastructure improvements, or more contemporary, such as long-term sharing of the costs of infrastructure maintenance or other traditionally public services, or the creation of community-building amenities, such as plazas, parks, and open space, public art, or bikeways.

Successful Public/Private Partnerships:
From Principles to Practice (ULI, 2016)

Balsley Park | New York, New York
Courtesy of Thomas Balsley Associates

NEW YORK CITY PRIVATELY OWNED PUBLIC SPACE PROGRAM

The New York City Privately Owned Public Space Program began in 1961 to encourage private developers to create spaces for public use in exchange for allowing greater project density—including through additional building area or relief from height and setback restrictions. Since the program began, developers have created more than 3.5 million square feet of public space, including plazas, arcades, open-air concourses, and covered pedestrian spaces.

The city of New York notes that "an impressive amount of public space has been created in parts of the city with little access to public parks....Some spaces have proved to be valuable public resources, but others are inaccessible or devoid of the kinds of amenities that attract public use."

In 2007, a zoning text amendment updated the design standards for New York City's privately owned public plazas to encourage higher-quality public spaces that are open and inviting at the sidewalk, more accessible, provide a sense of safety and security, and include places to sit.[45]

Before

After

Sheffield Plaza, now Balsley Park | New York, New York
Courtesy of Thomas Balsley Associates

NOTES

1. National Recreation and Park Association, "Americans' Engagement with Parks Survey," accessed March 13, 2018, https://www.nrpa.org/publications-research/research-papers/Engagement/.

2. Austin G. Barrett, Nick Pitas, and Andrew Mowen, "First in Our Hearts but Not in Our Pocket Books: Trends in Local Governmental Financing for Parks and Recreation from 2004 to 2014," *Journal of Park and Recreation Administration* 35 (2017): 1–19.

3. Nicholas Pitas, Austin Barrett, Andrew Mowen, and Kevin Roth, "The Great Recession's Profound Impact on Parks and Recreation," *Parks & Recreation*, February 6, 2018, https://www.nrpa.org/parks-recreation-magazine/2018/february/the-great-recessions-profound-impact-on-parks-and-recreation/.

4. National Recreation and Park Association, "Revitalizing Inner City Parks: New Funding Options Can Address the Needs of Underserved Urban Communities," Issue Brief, accessed March 26, 2018, https://www.nrpa.org/contentassets/f768428a39aa4035ae55b2aaff372617/urban-parks.pdf.

5. John Surico, *A New Leaf: Revitalizing New York City's Aging Park Infrastructure* (New York: Center for an Urban Future, 2018), https://nycfuture.org/pdf/CUF_A_New_Leaf.pdf.

6. "10-Minute Walk Campaign," 10-Minute Walk Campaign, accessed December 10, 2017, https://www.10minutewalk.org/.

7. Zoe Rosenberg, "Tour Hunters Point South's Amenity-Packed Affordable Rentals,"   June 2, 2015, https://ny.curbed.com/2015/6/2/9954440/tour-hunters-point-souths-amenity-packed-affordable-rentals.

8. Richard Mitchell and Frank Popham. "Effect of exposure to natural environment on health inequalities: An observational population study." *The Lancet* 372 (2008): 1655–1660.

9. Office of the Mayor of New York City, "Mayor Bloomberg Opens Hunter's Point South Waterfront Park in Queens, Part of Major Affordable Housing Development," Office of the Mayor of New York City website, August 28, 2013, https://www1.nyc.gov/office-of-the-mayor/news/286-13/mayor-bloomberg-opens-hunter-s-point-south-waterfront-park-queens-of-major-affordable#/0.

10. National Recreation and Park Association, "Parks and Recreation: A True Health Solution," accessed March 13, 2018, https://www.nrpa.org/contentassets/b6a210130ff343369e74f52e5a0f48a8/health-wellness-poster-nrpa.pdf.

11. Emily Nonko, "Long Island City's Hunters Point South Phase 2 Is Back on Track," *Curbed New York*, November 17, 2017, https://ny.curbed.com/2017/11/17/16669744/long-island-city-affordable-housing-hunters-point-south.

12. Zoe Rosenberg, "Tour Hunters Point South's Amenity-Packed Affordable Rentals," *Curbed New York*, June 2, 2015, https://ny.curbed.com/2015/6/2/9954440/tour-hunters-point-souths-amenity-packed-affordable-rentals.

13. Teresa Mozur, "6 Reasons Why Parks Matter for Health," *Culture of Health Blog*, August 22, 2016, https://www.rwjf.org/en/blog/2016/08/6_reasons_why_parks.html.

14. Urban Land Institute, *America in 2015: A ULI Survey of Views on Housing, Transportation, and Community* (Washington, DC: Urban Land Institute, 2015).

15. George Mason University Center for Regional Analysis, "Promoting Parks and Recreation's Role in Economic Development," National Recreation and Park Association, May 2018, https://www.nrpa.org/publications-research/research-papers/promoting-parks-and-recreations-role-in-economic-development/.

16. "National Capital Account for London," Mayor of London/London Assembly, accessed March 11, 2018, https://www.london.gov.uk/what-we-do/environment/parks-green-spaces-and-biodiversity/green-infrastructure/natural-capital-account-london#acc-i-49961.

17. Jill Johnston, "Urban Green Space, Disparities & Health," National Institute of Environmental Health Sciences, Keck School of Medicine, University of Southern California, accessed July 13, 2018, https://www.niehs.nih.gov/research/supported/translational/peph/webinars/green_spaces/urban_green_space_disparities_and_health_508.pdf.

18. Urban Land Institute, *Building Healthy Places Toolkit: Strategies for Enhancing Health in the Built Environment* (Washington, DC: Urban Land Institute, 2015).

19. "National Capital Account for London," Mayor of London/London Assembly, accessed March 11, 2018, https://www.london.gov.uk/what-we-do/environment/parks-green-spaces-and-biodiversity/green-infrastructure/natural-capital-account-london#acc-i-49961.

20. Eugenia C. South, Bernadette C. Hohl, Michelle C. Kondo et al., "Effect of Greening Vacant Land on Mental Health of Community-Dwelling Adults: A Cluster Randomized Trial," *JAMA Network Open 018*, no. 1 (July 20, 2018): 3, doi:10.1001/jamanetworkopen.2018.0298.

21. Urban Land Institute, *Building Healthy Places Toolkit: Strategies for Enhancing Health in the Built Environment* (Washington, DC: Urban Land Institute, 2015).

22. "11th Street Bridge Park: Equitable Development Plan," 11th Street Bridge Park website, 2015, https://bridgepark.org/sites/default/files/Resources/EDP%20Final%20-%20UPDATED.pdf.

23. National Recreation and Park Association, "Revitalizing Inner City Parks: New Funding Options Can Address the Needs of Underserved Urban Communities," Issue Brief, accessed March 26, 2018, https://www.nrpa.org/contentassets/f768428a39aa4035ae55b2aaff372617/urban-parks.pdf.

24. Urban Land Institute, *Building Healthy Places Toolkit: Strategies for Enhancing Health in the Built Environment* (Washington, DC: Urban Land Institute, 2015).

25. Peter Harnick and Ben Welle, *From Fitness Zones to the Medical Mile: How Urban Park Systems Can Best Promote Health and Wellness* (Washington, DC: The Trust for Public Land, 2011), http://cloud.tpl.org/pubs/ccpe-health-promoting-parks-rpt.pdf.

26. Urban Land Institute, *Building Healthy Places Toolkit: Strategies for Enhancing Health in the Built Environment* (Washington, DC: Urban Land Institute, 2015).

27. Gensler and Urban Land Institute, "Open Space: An Asset without a Champion?," Gensler website, 2011, https://www.gensler.com/research-insight/gensler-research-institute/open-spaces-1.

28. Gensler and Urban Land Institute, "Open Space: An Asset without a Champion?," Gensler website, 2011, https://www.gensler.com/research-insight/gensler-research-institute/open-spaces-1.

29. Urban Land Institute, *America in 2015: A ULI Survey of Views on Housing, Transportation, and Community* (Washington, DC: Urban Land Institute, 2015).

30. National Recreation and Park Association, "Revitalizing Inner City Parks: New Funding Options Can Address the Needs of Underserved Urban Communities," Issue Brief, accessed March 26, 2018, https://www.nrpa.org/contentassets/f768428a39aa4035ae55b2aaff372617/urban-parks.pdf.

31. John Surico, *A New Leaf: Revitalizing New York City's Aging Park Infrastructure* (New York: Center for an Urban Future, 2018), https://nycfuture.org/pdf/CUF_A_New_Leaf.pdf.

32. National Recreation and Park Association, "Why Parks and Recreation Are Essential Public Services," January 2010, https://www.nrpa.org/uploadedFiles/nrpa.org/Advocacy/Resources/Parks-Recreation-Essential-Public-Services-January-2010.pdf.

33. National Recreation and Park Association, "Americans' Broad-Based Support for Local Recreation and Park Services: Results from a Nationwide Study," 2016, https://www.nrpa.org/uploadedFiles/nrpa.org/Publications_and_Research/Research/Park-Perception-Study-NRPA-summary.pdf.

34. "Guthrie Green Park," swa Group, accessed June 22, 2018, www.swagroup.com/projects/guthrie-green-park/.

35. Kyle Hinchey, "City Leaders Celebrate Guthrie Green's Success on Its Five-Year Anniversary," *Tulsa World*, September 1, 2017, https://www.tulsaworld.com/homepagelatest/city-leaders-celebrate-guthrie-green-s-success-on-its-five/article_9b210da1-47f8-528a-94ad-19aef87c63b8.html.

36. Deborah A. Cohen, Bing Han, Kathryn Pitkin Derose, Stephanie Williamson, Terry Marsh, Laura Raaen, and Thomas L. McKenzie, "The Paradox of Parks in Low-Income Areas: Park Use and Perceived Threats," *Environment and Behavior* 48, no. 1 (January 2016): 230–245, https://www.rand.org/pubs/external_publications/EP66281.html.

37. Daniel Lobo, "ULI Urban Open Space Award Finalists: Guthrie Green," Urban Land Institute, August 4, 2014, https://urbanland.uli.org/planning-design/uli-urban-open-space-awards-finalists-guthrie-green/.

38. Trust for Public Land, "Eight Ways Parks Improve Your Health," accessed July 23, 2018, https://www.tpl.org/file/eight-ways-parks-improve-your-health#sm.00001fflcuwx62dbushbm6713642s.

39. National Recreation and Park Association, "Parks and Recreation: A True Health Solution," accessed March 13, 2018, https://www.nrpa.org/contentassets/b6a210130ff343369e74f52e5a0f48a8/health-wellness-poster-nrpa.pdf.

40. Deborah A. Cohen, Bing Han, Catherine J. Nagel, Peter Harnik, Thomas L. McKenzie, Kelly R. Evenson et al., "The First National Study of Neighborhood Parks: Implications for Physical Activity," *American Journal of Preventive Medicine* 51, no. 4 (October 2016): 419–426, https://doi.org/10.1016/j.amepre.2016.03.021.

41. "Avalon Redefines Mixed-Use," North American Properties, accessed July 23, 2018, https://www.naproperties.com/places/avalon/.

42. Scott Sowers, "Real Estate Developers Become the Entertainers," *CityLab*, October 24, 2017, https://www.citylab.com/life/2017/10/mixed-use-developments-real-estate-entertainment-public-space/543711/.

43. Deborah A. Cohen, Kathryn Pitkin Derose, Bing Han, Stephanie Williamson, Terry Marsh, and Laura Raaen, *City of Los Angeles Neighborhood Parks: Research Findings and Policy Implications (2003–2015)* (Santa Monica, CA: RAND Corporation, 2016), https://www.rand.org/pubs/research_reports/RR1573.html.

44. Peter Harnick and Ben Welle, *From Fitness Zones to the Medical Mile: How Urban Park Systems Can Best Promote Health and Wellness* (Washington, DC: The Trust for Public Land, 2011), http://cloud.tpl.org/pubs/ccpe-health-promoting-parks-rpt.pdf.

45. New York City Department of City Planning, "New York City's Privately Owned Public Spaces," accessed June 9, 2018, https://www1.nyc.gov/site/planning/plans/pops/pops-history.page.

Guthrie Green | Tulsa, Oklahoma
Tom Fox

Grand Park | Los Angeles, California
Jim Simmons

Hunter's Point South | Queens, New York
Albert Vecerka Esto

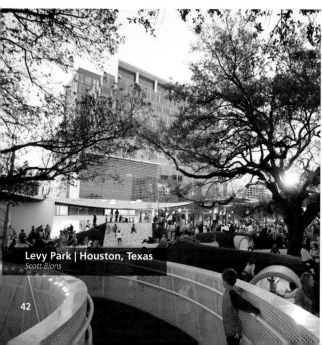

Levy Park | Houston, Texas
Scott Blons

Solaris Plaza | Vail, Colorado
Solaris

Katy Trail | Dallas, Texas
Lauren Whitson

ACKNOWLEDGMENTS

ULI is grateful to the Robert Wood Johnson Foundation for its support of this research.

We gratefully acknowledge the contributions of the following individuals:

Robin Baldock, executive director, Friends of the Katy Trail
Tom Balsley, principal, SWA/Balsley
Rachel Banner, senior program manager, National Recreation and Parks Association
Jonathan Brinsden, chief executive officer, Midway and ULI trustee
Sharon Cohn, president, Solaris Redevelopment Co.
Britton Church, vice president of development, JLB Partners
Stanton Doyle, senior program officer, George Kaiser Family Foundation
Adam Fenton, vice president of development, BMC Investments
Nicole Giangregorio, marketing and office manager, SWA/Balsley
Leonard Greco, vice president, New York City Economic Development Corporation
Alec Grossman, account coordinator, BerlinRosen
Fran Hegeler, director of marketing and communications, SWA Group
Jeff Hoffman, vice president of development, BMC Investments
Ken Levit, executive director, George Kaiser Family Foundation
Charlie McCabe, director, Center for City Park Excellence, Trust for Public Land
Tony Paradowski, partner, Superjacent; project designer for Grand Park
Sharon Roerty, senior program officer, Robert Wood Johnson Foundation
George Ruther, housing director and former director of community development, town of Vail
Charlie Singer, development analyst, East West Partners
Bill Tatham, photographer, SWA Group
Ann Taylor, senior vice president, Midway
Lauren Whitson, membership and marketing director, Friends of the Katy Trail
Shavone Williams, assistant vice president of public affairs, New York City Economic Development Corporation
Heather Wimberly, vice president of operations, Guthrie Green
Ann Zoller, senior adviser, Strategy Design Partners LLC